CELEBRATING THE CITY OF ATHENS

Celebrating the City of Athens

Walter the Educator

Silent King Books

SILENT KING BOOKS

SKB

Copyright © 2024 by Walter the Educator

All rights reserved. No part of this book may be reproduced in any manner whatsoever without written permission except in the case of brief quotations embodied in critical articles and reviews.

First Printing, 2024

Disclaimer
This book is a literary work; the story is not about specific persons, locations, situations, and/or circumstances unless mentioned in a historical context. Any resemblance to real persons, locations, situations, and/or circumstances is coincidental. This book is for entertainment and informational purposes only. The author and publisher offer this information without warranties expressed or implied. No matter the grounds, neither the author nor the publisher will be accountable for any losses, injuries, or other damages caused by the reader's use of this book. The use of this book acknowledges an understanding and acceptance of this disclaimer.

Celebrating the City of Athens is a little collectible souvenir book that belongs to the Celebrating Cities Book Series by Walter the Educator. Collect them all and more books at WaltertheEducator.com

USE THE EXTRA SPACE TO TAKE NOTES AND DOCUMENT YOUR MEMORIES

ATHENS

In the cradle of dawn where the Parthenon glows,

Celebrating the City of Athens

Athens awakens as the marbled light grows.

Ancient echoes resound through the modern day,

In the heart of a city where gods used to play.

Her streets whisper tales of glory and grace,

Of philosophers' wisdom and heroes' embrace.

Socrates wandered these pathways of thought,

Where democracy's seedlings were nurtured and taught.

Celebrating the City of Athens

Marble and stone tell stories so old,

Of battles and legends in times of bold.

The Agora hums with the life of the past,

Where traders and thinkers in dialogue amassed.

The olive trees stand, silent and wise,

Their leaves a testament to centuries' sighs.

Celebrating the City of Athens

Athena's breath in the rustling leaves,

A city where time like a river weaves.

Underneath the Acropolis, shadows dance,

In the footsteps of legends, we find our chance.

To trace the steps of those who came before,

Celebrating the City of
Athens

In Athens, the heart of wisdom's core.

The Panathenaic Stadium, gleaming and grand,

Witness to the feats of a bygone land.

Where athletes raced and crowds would cheer,

Their spirit remains, ever vibrant, ever near.

In the labyrinth of Plaka, with its charm,

Every corner holds a historic alarm.

Cobblestone streets with stories to tell,

Of a city's endurance, its rise, and its swell.

From the heights of Lycabettus, gaze afar,

To the sprawling city, where ancient and modern spar.

A skyline etched with tales untold,

In Athens, the present and past unfold.

The blue Aegean, a whispering muse,

Celebrating the City of
Athens

Inspiring poets, igniting their fuse.

From Piraeus port, the ships set sail,

Carrying dreams on the mythic gale.

The spirit of Dionysus lives in the air,

In festivals and feasts, laughter and care.

The theatres echo with plays profound,

In Athens, where culture and art are crowned.

Celebrating the City of Athens

ABOUT THE CREATOR

Walter the Educator is one of the pseudonyms for Walter Anderson. Formally educated in Chemistry, Business, and Education, he is an educator, an author, a diverse entrepreneur, and he is the son of a disabled war veteran. "Walter the Educator" shares his time between educating and creating. He holds interests and owns several creative projects that entertain, enlighten, enhance, and educate, hoping to inspire and motivate you.

Follow, find new works, and stay up to date with Walter the Educator™
at WaltertheEducator.com

www.ingramcontent.com/pod-product-compliance
Lightning Source LLC
LaVergne TN
LVHW052007060526
838201LV00059B/3893